We All Have Our Challenges

for Kelsey Mathes with my good wishes
thoughts and prayers. May you
continue to be an integral part
of the Universal Mosaic and of
my "family by choice" Joe P

We All Have Our Challenges
Bits of Wisdom

By
Liliya Bromberg

With Special Help From
Ryan G. Beale

This book will be available in quantity at special
discounts for educators, organizations and retail
distribution through the INGRAM Book Company.
www.ingramcontent.com

Copyright © 2013 by Detroit Sparks, LLC
www.detroitsparks.com
First Edition: June 2013
Printed in the United States of America
ISBN: 978-0-98924-600-2

As told by Liliya Bromberg
With special help by Ryan G. Beale

Thank You

The support that I have received from the Friendship Circle has been amazing. When I first got sick, Bassie Shemtov and countless other people helped me and guided me throughout this whole process. I would be lost without their support.

Kids of Courage is an organization that takes the sickest kids on trips and allows them to enjoy their life even if they have chronic illnesses. These trips have helped relieve my stress and nerves during some of the hardest times in my life.

These organizations have given myself and countless others amazing friendship, support and encouragement.

My friends' love, their texts, their calls and their kindness are what make me feel like any other human being. I thank G-d for them everyday.

I am thankful for the patience, love and support that my parents have unwaveringly given me throughout my life.

It is the messengers that keep me alive. - Liliya

We each have a story behind us. A story filled with overcoming challenges that is filled with fear, anxiety and stress. We have to overcome those obstacles in order to find hope.

I am 22 years old and I have a lot of days where I am nervous because I do not know what is going to happen to me in the future. Being such a young age, I understand that I am being challenged for a reason.

Prayer, reflection, G-d and warm hearts are what give me hope and continued faith.

I take life day-by-day, hour-by-hour, because you never know where life is going to take you.

I Am Thankful

The one thing that I do everyday is thank G-d.
I am thankful to be alive because my life is day-by-day
and hour-by-hour.

This really is the only way to live because
G-d is the only one who knows what tomorrow will bring.

Twenty-Two

People my age don't often appreciate living in the moment. They tend to take advantage of their time. They take things for granted until they are forced to face the reality that we are powerless to know what tomorrow really brings.

Always Be Thankful

Remember, we all go through challenges in life regardless of what we are ever diagnosed with. Remember there is always someone else who has to fight harder and has to be stronger than you do.

Make A Choice

Life is full of challenges and unexpected things, but
throughout my lifetime I have had to battle a very
serious illness, which I have
chosen to make me stronger and wiser.

Be Flexible

Although many people are very good planners, truthfully nobody knows what tomorrow will actually bring.

Have Faith

Challenges can be overcome through faith in G-d,
prayer and with confidence that you are
where you are supposed to be.

Feel The Love

I've gone on a lot of trips and done a lot of things over the years and that has been very nice. However, simple things such as pictures work as reminders that I am loved; even just an email from a friend helps me realize that people that I don't get to see often miss me. Those feelings of love are what keep me going.

Capture The Moments

Take pictures of the world around you even though people may think you're crazy. It's those courageous picture-taking moments that allow you to relive those moments later in life. Looking back at those special pictures makes me feel so good. Life is too short not to enjoy good moments over and over!

Parents vs. Friends

Parents and friends are two different categories.
Parents care with their deepest emotions, while friends
give you the interactions you need and
allow you to just be your age.

The Support of Friends

When I got diagnosed with cancer, I was extremely scared at first. The doctors did a 5-hour surgery on me. They were shocked by my strength and will to fight. I owe that to the amazing friends that stood by me. Without them I don't know how strong I would have been or would be today.

Quick Bits

Life is a day-by-day process.

Everybody has a little bit of magic inside of them, no matter where they are in life.

No matter what G-d ends up throwing at me, the power of friendship always helps me to keep fighting.

More Quick Bits

Thanks to technology, age and distance don't matter at this point as much as anything else.

I am horribly afraid of MRI's...because I can never sit still, maybe they can work on this a little bit.

Friends texting me helps my anxiety at times. I am thankful for every one of them and every single day of life that I am given.

Turn It Up

One thing that does help me is music. If I have nothing
else around me, it relaxes me in a way
that allows me to unwind.

Music

I have a lot of friends that can play piano, but I like
hearing a good guitar once in awhile.

Look Deeper

People should look deeper into their purpose before G-d throws them a challenge that makes you realize that life isn't just about you.

It's about thinking of others before yourself.

Who Is This About?

**If you don't think about others,
what kind of life are you living?**

Let's Be Real

Until you wake up and realize that you're going to the bathroom in a bag and can't feed yourself, you never realize how lucky you are to live or what you could have possibly given to others when you had your health. That is what life is about.

Think Small

It's the smallest things in life that we should be thankful for and appreciative of.

Journal and Reflect

When I get my feelings out on paper I feel much better.

Have Faith Even When It's Hard

I am absolutely positive there is a reason why I have this
cancer for a second time...
and I'm still trying to figure it out.

Be a Better Friend

It is the ongoing messages that I share between friends and loved ones that keeps me going and keeps me fighting when I feel like giving up.

Fight With Spirit

Even the doctors whom beat my body up have come to understand that the fight is more than just physical, it is spiritual.

Build Your Peace Of Mind

Serenity has given me the strength, courage and wisdom to know the difference of which battles are worth fighting.

Friendship

Friends are the siblings that G-d intended for us.

Stay Faithful

One thing that I have learned is to never give up hope.

No Pain, No Gain

The harder you have to battle, the more good things will come from within those challenges.

Appreciate Every Day

Never take your life for granted because we never know
what is going to happen to us.

Our Lives Are Like A Candle

Our lives are like a candle burning down with a bright flame. Our soul is the flame, powerfully emanating light that can transcend.

The wax of the candle represents G-d protecting us 24/7 regardless of where we are. Even if we think that the candle has burned out,
it never really is extinguished.

The strength and the light of the candle can represent a million things; hope is just one part within the essence of the flame that is always ascending.

Your Flame Can Start A Fire

We all have a foundation to build within ourselves, which
then transfers to others and that is what
the light of the candle represents.

Nervousness and Fear Quick Bits

Nervousness comes from being afraid and allowing fear to sit in our minds.

We all have some fear at one point or another.

Fear is when you are scared of something that you don't understand or when you don't know what the future holds.

Fear is also the emotion that we feel right before we learn to accept that we cannot control all of the circumstances in our lives.

Music Helps

I am scared of the dark because I am nervous of what
the darkness may bring, therefore I listen to music,
which often helps to soothe my mind.

Be You!

Walking in someone else's shoes means that you must *really* feel what another person goes through.

Sometimes when your own shoes are too heavy, it is ok to break down and cry… it helps to get rid of some of the extra weight that you are carrying.

As much as we try, we never can truly understand what it is like to walk in another person's shoes.

My Heart Is Like Yours

There are people that I know that deal with different things in their lives, however my friends have learned from my perspective, that being in a chair and having a unique illness does not prevent me from experiencing the same emotions that everyone else does.

Everyone Holds a Gift In Which You Must Unlock

Interactions, to me, means giving someone a chance to be like every other person in the world.

When people interact with me without judging the fact that I am in a chair, the fact that I have CP or a very rare form of cancer, not only do I appreciate it, but I see it as an opportunity to leave them with a perspective that can possibly empower them for the rest of their lives.

Genuine interactions with good-hearted people allow me to temporarily feel relieved of my own challenges.

Cross Roads

Our lives consist of long roads. Every single person in life has a road to travel but at points, it cracks.

It takes a person with good vision, good coaches and a strong will to fight, that allows them to overstep the cracks and their own boundaries. Then, they can continue along their paths and learn to overcome the challenges within their own lives.

Many people do not realize this concept because they try to hide the fact that they are being challenged and are afraid to confront their own cracks along their road.

It's Not Supposed To Always Be Easy

Real life is not easy.
People try to mix up their real life issues that they need
to confront with their personal issues to intentionally
confuse themselves to avoid facing reality.

Doctors

Doctors fight to save lives or at least they do their best. My doctors have been very nice and give me support, both physically and mentally.

Doctors sometimes have to give bad news, but with a little faith and follow through of the doctor's orders we can increase our ability to live a healthier life.

Being Physically Challenged

Just because I am in a chair or the fact that someone may be disabled does not mean that they cannot accomplish beautiful things in their life. There is always hope and there is always purpose to find in the world.

Being physically challenged doesn't mean that you can't achieve more things in your life, just because of a diagnosis. It does not mean that you are unable to succeed. It just means that you have to find new ways and new definitions for how to define success.

Life's Inner Beauty

Life is a long road that gives us all kinds of challenges. Being physically challenged just means that we have to strive harder and focus a little more of our energy on our inner beauty.

Remove Your Fear

Sometimes, I myself get stressed out because I am nervous or scared, but it does not mean that I can't find the courage to survive.

Make Goals

One should set goals for themselves. Once you set goals for yourself, you should not stop believing in them, even when life throws you distractions.

Keep Your Goals

No matter where you go or what you do,
your goals can be accomplished in your life.

Even when you don't have your full health, you can still
set goals, however it is easier to set your goals before
you have to deal with your health.

Achieving your goals within your life can be
accomplished with a strong sense of belief.

Technology and Bowling

With the amount of technology that we have in the world today, it is easier to get in touch with people, to connect and it allows us to have abilities to connect to friends and family both near and far.

Between my electric chair and the electric scoreboard at the alley, I now consider myself a competitive bowler. Thank G-d for my insurance so I can afford to take advantage of this modern technology.

Bowling once a week has given me something that I can regularly look forward to. It's a time to get out of the house and connect with other like-minded friends.

Art

Art is extremely therapeutic.
I have found that painting and scrapbooking keeps my mind busy and removes me from focusing on negative things that I have to confront in my life.

Music and Art

Music and art open a completely new part of my mind that I find to be a very comfortable place to relax in.

There are different types of art. I have always considered myself to be a crafty person. What I like about art is that it is nonjudgmental; it does not discriminate young or old, talented or not so talented. Art is a process, just like life is a process.

Go For More Walks

Whenever I go on a walk, 90% of the time I see my friends who show me love. When it is nice out we take advantage of going outside because the fresh air helps me breathe easier.

When you stay in your house, you can get lazy and stuck.

Call a good friend and go on walks more often. I promise you will not regret it.

Feel The Air

The fresh air allows me to breathe easier.
It makes me feel like a new person as soon I get outside.

I have found that the air in different cities makes me feel
different. So far, the air in northern California has been
my favorite, although I don't have too many places to
compare it too.

The Beauty Of Horses

I have always found horses to be very therapeutic and healing. I miss going horseback riding these days because of my health, however I would advise others to learn to appreciate horses and horseback riding for it's unique benefits. The efforts of the 4H organization had helped to allow me to experience this wonderful opportunity.

Visualize

If you imagine that you will be healthier and better,
then it can happen.

Healing

I'm a quick healer when it comes to the challenges that have been placed upon me.

Healing is a connection between your mind, your body and G-d.

You have to relax your mind in order to heal.

Check Your Pulse

If life does not throw you distractions, you have to do a double check to see if you are *really* living.

We each have a story behind us.
A story filled with overcoming challenges that is filled
with fear, anxiety and stress. We have to overcome
those obstacles in order to find hope.

CPSIA information can be obtained
at www.ICGtesting.com
Printed in the USA
LVHW081003251022
731510LV00017B/207

9 780989 246002